EXPLORING THE CRESTON VALLEY

EXPLORING THE CRESTON VALLEY

Tanna Patterson-Z

Published by Waterwheel Press, Vancouver

Canadian Cataloguing in Publication Data

Patterson, Tanna Lea, 1955-
   Exploring the Creston Valley

   ISBN 0-920641-14-8

   1. Walking - British Columbia - Creston Valley
- Guide-books. 2. Cycling - British Columbia
- Creston Valley - Guide-books. 3. Canoes and
canoeing - British Columbia - Creston Valley
- Guide-books. 4. Trails - British Columbia
- Creston Valley - Guide-books. 5. Creston Valley
(B.C.) - Description and travel - Guide-books.
I. Title.
FC3845.C75A3 1989   917.11'4   C89-091556-3
F1089.C75P3 1989

Printed and bound in Canada by Hignell Printing Limited

Dedicated to

Gene and Jan,
my fellow weekend adventurers

Contents

Part One: Canoeing

Part Two: Bicycling

Part Three: Walking

List of Maps

Acknowledgements

Brian Stushnoff and Staff
Creston Valley Wildlife Management Authority

Bob Purdy, Coordinator
Creston Valley Wildlife Centre

Lower Kutenai Band
Thank you for passage through band land

Monte Chan
biologist, naturalist, proofreader

Carl Jones
historian, Creston Valley Museum Society

Vern Petersen
Thank you for parking on private property

Ed McMackin
biologist, naturalist

Gail Greenwood
Creston Chamber of Commerce

Betsy Brierly
proofreader

Town of Creston
Thank you for maps

Photographers:

Ken Alexander, Patti Kaye
Ralph McKone, George Brown
Irma Sleik, Betsy Brierly

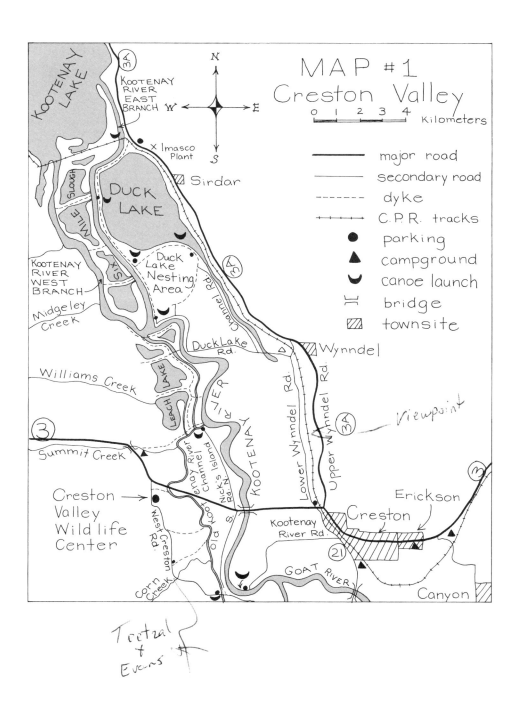

MAP # 1
Creston Valley

0 1 2 3 4 Kilometers

——————	major road
————	secondary road
- - - - -	dyke
+—+—+	C.P.R. tracks
●	parking
▲	campground
☽	canoe launch
⊓	bridge
▨	townsite

KOOTENAY LAKE

KOOTENAY RIVER EAST BRANCH

X Imasco Plant

▨ Sirdar

SLOUGH

SIX MILE

DUCK LAKE

KOOTENAY RIVER WEST BRANCH

Duck Lake Nesting Area

Channel Rd.

Midgeley Creek

DuckLake Rd.

▨ Wynndel

Williams Creek

LEACH LAKE

RIVER

KOOTENAY

Lower Wynndel Rd.

Upper Wynndel Rd.

Viewpoint

3

Summit Creek

Kootenay River Channel

Nick's Island Rd. N.

Creston Valley Wildlife Center

West Creston Rd.

Old Kootenay River

Erickson

Creston

Kootenay River Rd.

21

Corn Creek

GOAT RIVER

Canyon

Tretza & Evans

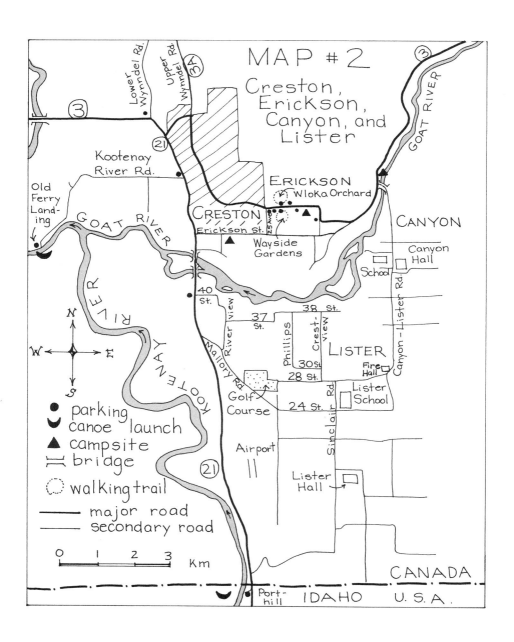

MAP #2
Creston,
Erickson,
Canyon, and
Lister

Lower Wynndel Rd.
Upper Wynndel Rd.
3A
3
GOAT RIVER
21
Kootenay River Rd.
ERICKSON
Wloka Orchard
Old Ferry Landing
GOAT RIVER
CRESTON
Erickson St.
25 Ave
CANYON
Canyon Hall
School
Wayside Gardens
40 St.
River View
37 St.
38 St.
Phillips
Crest-view
Canyon–Lister Rd.
Mallory Rd.
LISTER
Fire Hall
30 St.
28 St.
Lister School
Golf Course
24 St.
Sinclair Rd.
Airport
Lister Hall

N
W   E
S

● parking
☾ canoe launch
▲ campsite
⊐⊏ bridge
◌ walking trail
— major road
— secondary road

0   1   2   3   Km

CANADA
☾ Port-hill   IDAHO   U.S.A.

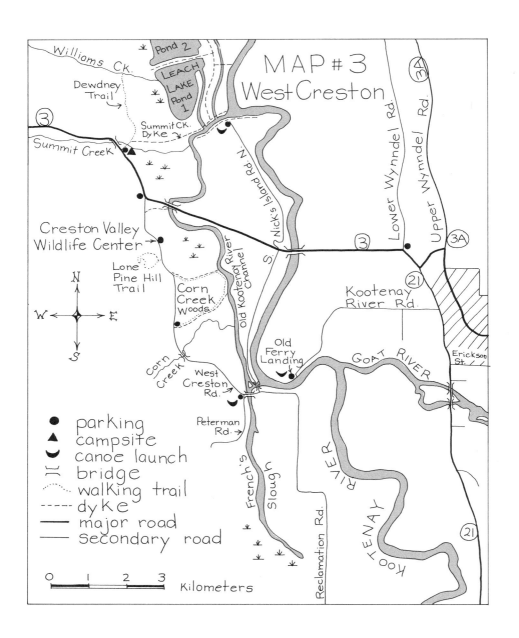

MAP #3
West Creston

Williams Ck.

Pond 2

LEACH LAKE

Pond 1

Dewdney Trail

Summit CK. Dyke

3

Summit Creek

3A

Lower Wynndel Rd.

Upper Wynndel Rd.

Nick's Island Rd. N.

Creston Valley Wildlife Center

Lone Pine Hill Trail

Corn Creek Woods

Old Kootenay River Channel

S.

3

3A

21

Kootenay River Rd.

N
W ← → E
S

Old Ferry Landing

GOAT RIVER

Erickson St.

Corn Creek

West Creston Rd.

Peterman Rd.

French's Slough

Reclamation Rd.

KOOTENAY RIVER

21

● parking
▲ campsite
☽ canoe launch
II bridge
⋯⋯ walking trail
----- dyke
── major road
── secondary road

0   1   2   3
Kilometers

12

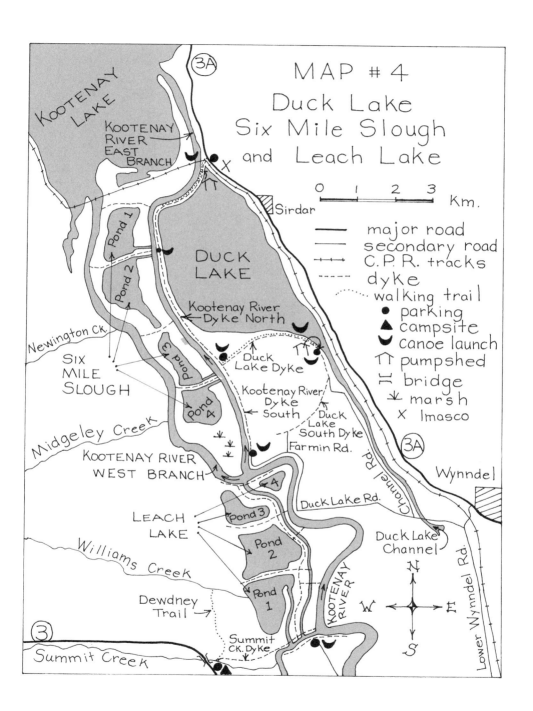

MAP # 4
Duck Lake
Six Mile Slough
and Leach Lake

KOOTENAY LAKE

KOOTENAY RIVER EAST BRANCH

Sirdar

0 1 2 3 Km.

—— major road
═══ secondary road
+—+ C.P.R. tracks
----- dyke
······ walking trail
● parking
▲ campsite
◡ canoe launch
⇑ pumpshed
⊐ bridge
↓ marsh
X Imasco

Pond 1

Pond 2

DUCK LAKE

Kootenay River Dyke North

Newington Ck.

Pond 3

SIX MILE SLOUGH

Duck Lake Dyke

Pond 4

Kootenay River Dyke South

Kootenay River Dyke South

Duck Lake South Dyke

Midgeley Creek

KOOTENAY RIVER WEST BRANCH

Farmin Rd.

3A

Wynndel

Duck Lake Rd.

LEACH LAKE

Pond 3

Pond 2

Channel Rd.

Duck Lake Channel

Williams Creek

Pond 1

N

Dewdney Trail →

KOOTENAY RIVER

W   E

3

Summit Ck. Dyke

S

Lower Wynndel Rd.

Summit Creek

13

MAP #5
Town of Creston
N.T.S.

• Parking   ▲ Campsite
① Schikurski Park
② Centennial Park
③ Kinsman Park
④ Don Burns Park
⑤ Swimming Pool
⑥ Tennis Courts
⑦ Library
⑧ Museum
⑨ Labatt's Brewery
   (Kokanee)
🌳 Orchard

Part One
Canoeing

1. Six Mile Slough

Six Mile Slough is a series of 4 ponds located between the east and west branches of the Kootenay River. The ponds are separated from each other by grass-covered dykes. By opening or closing portals in the dykes, the Wildlife Management Authority can adjust water levels in each pond to benefit the waterfowl. The ponds are shallow bodies of standing water rich in cattails, reeds, and sedges. This is ideal waterfowl habitat, so if you want to paddle around looking at ducks and muskrats, this is the place. Canoeists are encouraged to maintain a safe distance from the waterfowl during the nesting months of May, June, and July because any disturbances may be detrimental to successful reproduction and rearing of young chicks.

Portaging enables you to reach the ponds and pass from one pond to the next. Remember which pond you are exploring and what your access point is.

Getting There

See Map 1—Follow Hwy 3 west from Creston, turning right 0.2 km past the junction of Hwy 3 and Hwy 21 onto the Lower Wynndel Road. Turn left onto Duck Lake Road 6.9 km later. Watch for this sudden turn because it is not well marked. Travel 1.2 km past the giant, pyramidal greenhouse and turn north onto Channel Road at Arnold's Strawberry Farm.

See Map 4—Follow Channel Road for 5.5 km until a pump-shed appears on the right side of the road across from a small parking area. From this point on, you are on a dyke that borders the south end of Duck Lake. The dyke is wide enough for only one vehicle, with few places to pull over to let a second vehicle pass. Follow the dyke its entire length, 3 km. This dyke meets another dyke at a T-junction. Beyond the T is the east branch of the Kootenay River. Unload and launch the canoe here and park your vehicle in a small lot just below the T, toward Duck Lake.

On The Water

The river moves slowly northward to Kootenay Lake. To reach the closest pond, Pond 3, paddle south from the launch a very short distance, 0.2 km. Cross the river and pull up on the bank at a place marked by the absence of trees. This is where a dyke from Six Mile Slough meets the river.

Portage over the dyke, down to a narrow channel about 1 m wide. You must make a second portage around a fallen footbridge in the channel. This waterway leads to Pond 3 of Six Mile Slough.

The water around the pond's perimeter is deeper than the water in the middle, where pond vegetation is prolific. At times, the middle areas may be too shallow for a canoe.

To launch closer to Ponds 1 and 2, use the second canoe launch located 5.6 km north of the T-junction on the Kootenay River Dyke. Travel north along the dyke and park on the west side near the launch (see Map 1 or 4). Launch the canoe and follow the current of the river northward a number of metres until the dyke is sighted. Portage up the bank and down the other side. Pond 1 is on the north side of the dyke, Pond 2 on the south side.

Resting in the open water of Six Mile Slough, you may see tundra swans, white-fronted geese, gadwalls, pintails, redheads, common goldeneye, bufflehead, and flocks of greater and lesser scaup. The ponds are a sea of red in June and July when the water smartweed is in bloom.

Distance: Approximately 10 km (6 miles) of waterway.

Time: 10 minutes to cross the river, 10 minutes to portage over the dykes. The amount of time on the water depends on amount of exploring you want to do.

Parking: T-junction where Duck Lake Dyke meets Kootenay River Dyke at the southwest corner of Duck Lake, OR 5.6 km north on Kootenay River Dyke from T-junction on west side of Duck Lake.

Maps: See Maps 1 and 4.

Photographs: Six Mile Slough - Middle Area of Pond 3—T. Patterson-Z.

Note: Wildlife Management Unit land is open to hunters during the autumn hunting season, September to December.

Six Mile Slough   Middle Area of Pond 3

2. Kootenay River—
East Branch to Midgeley's cabin

Here is a beautiful stretch of quiet river enclosed by heavily forested banks. Osprey, eagle, great blue heron, and their nesting areas make this canoe route very special. The river is slow-moving, clean, and free of rapids; however, the steep, wooded banks are slippery and sometimes rocky, leaving few places to pull a canoe onto the shore. No picnic, recreation areas, or garbage cans exist. The only bar on this river is the occasional sand bar. The river continues to flow northward to Kootenay Lake for 10 km. Unless you are an experienced canoeist familiar with this area, refrain from venturing into Kootenay Lake. Storms can appear suddenly. Strong winds, rough water, and the scarcity of boat-to-shore accesses make a bad combination.

Stopping at a sand bar just before Midgeley Creek enters the river mixes exploring with canoeing, and results in an interesting afternoon.

Getting There

See Map 1—Travel west along Hwy 3 and turn right 0.2 km past the junction of Hwy 3 and Hwy 21 onto Lower Wynndel Road. Drive for 6.9 km along Lower Wynndel Road and turn left onto Duck Lake Road. Note mileage.

See Map 4—Travel along Duck Lake Road for 3.6 km past the pyramidal greenhouse and past the Channel Road turn-off. The road soon turns to gravel. Duck Lake Road curves to the right 3.6 km from its start and follows the Kootenay River Dyke. At 5.6 km, the road passes a cluster of haysheds at Farmin Road. Here the road narrows as you climb the dyke that borders the Kootenay River. At 6.8 km, stop at a clearing on the left. Note the faded red and white, wooden power poles. There is a small parking area here and an excellent canoe launch. You are looking at the east branch of the Kootenay River. The current is flowing northward.

On The Water

Launch and paddle south against the current for about 1 km until the main body—the west branch—of the Kootenay River appears. Stay right, and paddle with the current. Notice that the current has increased in strength.

After 1/2 hour of leisurely paddling, or approximately 2 km, look for a sandy, low-lying area on the left. This is one of the rare places on the river where the banks give way, presenting an access to the shore. This low spot, located before the confluence of Midgeley Creek and the Kootenay River, is not clearly visible and can easily be overlooked. Sometimes this low area is too marshy to beach a canoe. In this case, paddle a little farther down the river to where the river bends to the north. There is a sandy bank on the west side of the river with a small amount of level ground in front of it. The climb to the top of the bank is steep and loose. Try to avoid grappling with the rosebushes. Once the canoe has been grounded, you can explore the area and get involved with some of the Valley's history.

The break in the steep bank was used as a boat access in the 1860s by the early settlers who no doubt learned of its location from the Kutenai Indians; the Kutenai travelled these waterways extensively in their Kutenai canoes long before the 1860s. Creston Valley's first white settler, David McLaughlin, had a ferry that crossed here. Only a spool that a rope or cable wrapped around remains of the ferry. This spool is displayed at the Creston Museum with a picture of a ferry similar to the original in design. The ferry was an integral part of the all-Canadian route mapped out by Edgar Dewdney in 1865. His mission was to join Fort Hope (present-day Hope) to the gold camps of Wild Horse Creek (near present-day Cranbrook).

Farther up the bank, before Midgeley Creek, is a meadow and a steep rise. The cabin that is intact between the meadow and the river belonged at the turn of the century to a man called Midgeley. Midgeley owned a steamboat that used to transport people, cattle, and logs up and down the west branch of the river. A gasoline engine, the only remnant of Midgeley's steamboat, has been hauled up onto the bank by local historian Carl Jones. Apparently, Mr. Midgeley was not liked by all. In the late 1920s, his body was found wrapped and anchored with chains to the bottom of the river, not far from his cabin.

Allow adequate time for your return from Midgeley's cabin; you will be going against the current for most of the route. Do not forget to turn left onto the east branch to reach the canoe launch.

Distance: 5 km return 2 1/2 km to Midgeley's Cabin.

Time: Estimate 4 km per hour, 1 1/2 hours.

Difficulty: Moderate. Return route is against current. Few access points on the river.

Access: From Kootenay River Dyke to the east branch of the Kootenay River.

Canoeing

Parking: On Kootenay River Dyke at the end of Duck Lake Road.

Maps: See Maps 1 and 4.

Photographs: Western Shore of Kootenay River—T. Patterson-Z.

Note: Wildlife Management Unit land is open to hunters during the autumn hunting season, September to December.

Western Shore of Kootenay River

3. Kootenay River—
East Branch to train bridge

The east branch of the Kootenay River is smaller and quieter than the west branch; you will see more wildlife and waterfowl, including a heron rookery where the river bends. Thirty or more bulky nests made of branches, twigs, reeds and grasses are located in the upper levels of the old cottonwood trees. The noisy, long-legged birds are easily observed at nesting time in April when the leaves are not yet on the trees. By June, the birds have flown from their nests, but they remain in and around the open shallow water of Duck Lake and along the margins of the Kootenay River until late summer. The Wildlife Centre has an excellent video about the life and habits of great blue herons called "A Heron Named Bill."

Getting There

Two vehicles are needed if you plan to travel only one way. Park one vehicle at the small pull-off on Hwy 3A, 0.2 km past the Imasco rock-crushing plant. (Hwy 3A heads north from Creston toward the Kootenay Lake Ferry and Nelson. See Map 4.) The pull-off is 12 km from Wynndel or 2.8 km from the Sirdar General Store. Take the other vehicle to the canoe launch.

See Map 1—To reach the canoe launch from Creston, turn right onto Lower Wynndel Road from Hwy 3, then turn left 6.9 km later onto Duck Lake Road. If you are returning from parking the first vehicle on Hwy 3A, turn right off of Hwy 3A onto the Lower Wynndel Road just before Wynndel. Turn right onto Duck Lake Road 0.5 km later.

See Map 4—Pass by the giant, pyramidal greenhouse. Turn right onto Channel Road at Arnold's Strawberry Farm. Follow Channel Road for 5.5 km to the pump-house. From here, follow Duck Lake Dyke its entire length, about 3 km, to a T-junction at Kootenay River Dyke. There are two launch sites on the Kootenay River Dyke.

On The Water

Launch 1 is at the T-junction. Unload the canoe and park in a small area just below the T, toward Duck Lake. From here, it is 8.6 km to the termination point at the C.P.R. train bridge.

23

Launch 2 is about 5.6 km farther north on the Kootenay River Dyke. The dyke road is narrow with overhanging shrubs; there are few places to pass an oncoming vehicle. The parking area at the second launch is very small. The approach is steep, grassy, and slippery when wet. From here the train trestle is only 3 km down river; the heron rookery, about half way to the trestle.

The trees along the east branch host a number of bird species besides the great blue heron. Look for grey catbird, yellow warbler, eastern kingbird, Swainson's thrush, western tanager, cedar waxwing, American kestrel, and osprey. Enjoy the music of the songbirds hidden in the trees as you drift downstream.

The pull-out area is just past the train bridge on the east side of the river. The river continues for another 3 km to Kootenay Lake. Once grounded, you have a portage of a few hundred metres along a well-gravelled road up to Hwy 3A where the first vehicle is located.

Distance: Launch 1 to Train Bridge, 8.6 km. Launch 2 to Train Bridge, 3 km.

Time: Estimate 4 km per hour. Launch 1, 2 1/4 hrs. Launch 2, 3/4 hr.

Difficulty: Easy. A slight current. Banks are steep and wooded, and not readily accessible.

Canoe Access: 2 launch sites on Kootenay River Dyke.

Parking: Park one vehicle at the small pull-off on Hwy 3A, 0.2 km past Imasco. Park second vehicle at Kootenay River Dyke.

Maps: See Maps 1 and 4.

Photographs: Canoe at Launch 1, Kootenay River east branch—T. Patterson-Z.; Herons nesting in trees, Kootenay River east branch— C.V.W.M.A.

Note: Wildlife Management Unit land is open to hunters during the autumn hunting season, September to December.

Canoe at Launch 1, Kootenay River east branch

Herons nesting in trees, Kootenay River east branch

25

4. Old Kootenay River Channel

The Old Kootenay River Channel, the stretch of water left behind when the present Kootenay River took a new path long ago, is a quiet, scenic waterway. The current is minimal; the depth is seldom more than a paddle's length; and the banks are accessible to a canoe in most places. The giant, aged poplar trees and the thick shrubbery along the banks are conducive to wildlife watching. Perch and bass are as plentiful as local fishermen on the bridge claim. This is a safe place to canoe. Bring the kids.

Getting There

See Map 3—Following Hwy 3 west from Creston, cross the Kootenay River Bridge and turn left onto Nick's Island South Road at the gas station. Drive for 3.8 km and cross a small wooden bridge. From the bridge you can see the Channel enter the Kootenay River. At the T-junction, turn right onto West Creston Road and cross a second wooden bridge. Both bridges pass over the Old Kootenay River Channel. There is a small parking area on the shoulder of West Creston Road just before the second bridge, but continue over the second bridge and turn left at Peterman Road to unload the canoe first. There is no dock at the Peterman Road access, but the bank is grassy and not very steep.

From mid-July to mid-September, the Old Kootenay River Channel gets very shallow. At times, it may not even be navigable. The water level depends upon the dams in the West Kootenay and the dam on the Kootenay River at Libby, Montana. The amount of water released by the dams, especially in summer when the demand is high, affects the canoeability of the Old Kootenay River Channel.

Water levels in the Channel return to normal by mid-September. If water levels in the Old Kootenay River Channel are not high enough to permit passage, try French's Slough to the south of the bridge as an excellent alternative. French's Slough is deeper water at the upper end of the Channel, but it has the same kind of slow-moving water suitable for novice canoeists.

On the Water

Once in the water, paddle toward the bridge. Beware of the dive-bombing cliff swallows whose mud nests are clearly visible from your vantage point underneath the bridge. After the bridge, the Channel splits temporarily. Keep left, maintaining a northern direction in order to keep within the Channel. If you follow the Channel to the right, it will take you under the first wooden bridge and into the Kootenay River.

Beyond the split, the Old Kootenay River Channel flows through land belonging to the Lower Kutenai Indian Band. After canoeing leisurely for 1/2 hour, you will notice Corn Creek entering the Channel.

After 3/4 hour paddling, or approximately 3 km, the Channel appears to branch again. Keep right, even though the passage appears to be blocked; this is a sharp bend where branches and fallen trees tend to collect. From here on, the land is owned by the Wildlife Management Area. Tacked up along the shores are nesting boxes for wood ducks, part of a Wildlife Management Unit project. You may want to return to your launch point from here.

The final 2.5 km of the Old Kootenay River Channel is travelled by naturalist- led canoes in the summer months. These canoe trips are operated through the Creston Valley Wildlife Centre and open to everyone for a small charge.

If you were to continue to Hwy 3, you would find removing a canoe at the bridge difficult. The terrain is marshy, and no parking is allowed on Hwy 3. Therefore, to reach a vehicle parked west of the Wildlife Centre turn-off, you must make a kilometre-long portage along the shoulder of the highway.

Distance: West Creston Road bridge to the sharp bend in the Channel, 6 km return; West Creston Road bridge to the Hwy 3 bridge, 11.2 km return.

Time: Estimate 4 km per hour, 1 1/2 hours (6 km return trip); 3 hours (11.2 km return trip.)

Difficulty: Easy. No Current. Shallow water. Accessible banks.

Canoe Access: From Peterman Road.

Parking: An extension of the shoulder of West Creston Road on west side of bridge. If disembarking at Hwy 3 bridge, park in the area about 1 km from the bridge, just west of the Wildlife Centre turn-off.

Photographs: Nick's Island Road South Bridge from Old Kootenay River Channel—T. Patterson-Z.

Note: Wildlife Management Unit land is open to hunters during the autumn hunting season, September to December.

Nick's Island Road South Bridge from Old Kootenay River Channel

5. French's Slough

This quiet section of water is not a slough, but a peaceful channel rich in wildlife: white-tailed deer come down to drink; beaver undertake home repairs; a frog sits on a lily pad; and a painted turtle may sun himself on a log. French's Slough is the upper end of the Old Kootenay River Channel, the stretch of water left behind when the Kootenay River formed its new course.

The current is minimal; the banks are accessible to canoe in most places; and the water remains deep enough in mid-summer to permit passage. The route is unhurried, scenic, and ideal for novice canoeists. This is the preferred alternative to the Old Kootenay River Channel north of the West Creston Bridge when the latter is too shallow to navigate.

Getting There

See Map 3—Follow Hwy 3 west from Creston, and cross the silver Kootenay River Bridge. Turn left onto Nick's Island South Road, travel for 3.8 km and cross a wooden bridge. You will be able to see the Old Kootenay River Channel join the Kootenay River from the bridge. At the T-junction, turn right onto West Creston Road. A second wooden bridge crosses over the Old Kootenay River Channel again. French's Slough is the stretch of water south of the bridge.

On The Water

Paddle south from the bridge, moving against the very slow-moving current. Keep right when the channel appears to fork. Large, old cottonwoods and thick shrubbery line the entire 5 km length of the waterway, a lush environment for wildlife.

Cliff swallows are plentiful around the bridge. Belted kingfishers, warblers, thrushes, flickers, woodpeckers, grouse, herons, owls and various dabbling waterfowl species may be spotted along the way. Songbirds are everywhere. Listen for their distinctive songs, and then try to spot them. Bird check-lists are available at the Creston Valley Wildlife Centre. The Centre always welcomes findings of new species and news of unusual numbers of a species. Photographs providing positive identification greatly assist researchers update the species list.

Birds are not the Slough's only inhabitants. Many animals, such as deer, coyote, mink, muskrat, marten, and beaver, also thrive in the area. The waterway itself is populated with perch, bass, and pumpkinseed.

The east side of the waterway is bordered by a dyke. At one time, farmers in the Creston Valley were forced to deal with annual flooding. Now, an elaborate system of dykes and the dam at Libby, Montana, control water excess in the Kootenay River. Spring flooding is no longer an aspect of farming in the Creston Valley.

Toward the end of the 5 km, the channel becomes quite marshy. Navigation may be difficult in the thick vegetation of late summer. Allow sufficient time for return.

Distance: 10 km return.

Time: Estimate 4 km per hour, 2 1/2 hours.

Difficulty: Easy. Little current. Accessible banks.

Canoe Access: From Peterman Road.

Parking: On extended shoulder of West Creston Road in front of bridge.

Map: See Map 3.

Photographs: Quiet Channelscape, French's Slough—Ken Alexander.

Note: Wildlife Management Unit land is open to hunters during the autumn hunting season, September to December.

Quiet Channelscape, French's Slough

6. Duck Lake
and Duck Lake Channel

This route offers open water or slow-moving, reedy waterway. Duck Lake provides the canoeist with many kilometres of open water; while Duck Lake Channel provides 6 km of quiet current and shore vegetation. Each habitat has its own resident wildlife and waterfowl.

Getting There

See Map 1—Turn right onto Lower Wynndel Road from Hwy 3 and travel for 6.9 km. Turn left onto Duck Lake Road. This intersection is not well marked, so watch for it. Once on Duck Lake Road, travel 1.2 km past the giant, pyramidal greenhouse. Turn north onto Channel Road at Arnold's Strawberry Farm, a place you will want to investigate in June, when the strawberries are in season.

See Map 4—Follow Channel Road for 5.5 km until a small pump-shed appears on the right side of the road. Across from the pump-shed is the small, unmarked parking area. From this point on, the road becomes part of Duck Lake Dyke bordering the south end of Duck Lake.

Duck Lake

To launch the canoe onto Duck Lake, continue along the dyke past the parking area. You can launch anywhere along the dyke because the water is very close to the roadway. Once the canoe is unloaded, you can park in the small parking area at the pump-shed or on one of the small pull-off areas along the dyke road.

A fairly calm, open lake, about 3 m deep, Duck Lake is suited to both diving ducks and dabbling ducks. It is one of the better birding locations in the Valley, especially during spring and fall migrations. The south end is more open than the north end, except where the Channel meets the Lake in the southeast corner. The man-made nesting platforms and boxes are securely hidden here amid the tall reeds and cattails.

In summer, the open water draws several species of waterfowl: gadwall, widgeon, pintail, redhead, ring-necked duck, flocks of scaup, goldeneye, bufflehead, and rafts of coots. Along the shoreline, look for the American avocet, which is identifiable by its long, upturned bill and lengthy bluish legs. The tundra swan is one of the migrant species that has appeared in great numbers in the past. Its presence has earned the Creston Valley the title "Valley of the Swans." In addition to the waterfowl seen on and around Duck Lake, there are black terns, killdeers, sandpipers, osprey, red-winged and yellow-headed blackbirds, and several species of shorebird. For a complete list of waterfowl species, see pages 71 and 72.

Duck Lake Channel

Park at the small area across the road from the pump-shed. Launch the canoe into the narrow channel of water that cuts through the reeds at the pump-shed. This is an excellent location for bird-watching in early spring. Because the water around the pump-shed is the first water to become ice-free, many species of birds gather together in a relatively small area.

Eventually the reeds and sedges give way to a tree-lined channel that continues south and east for about 5 km. The cottonwood trees and the shrubs on the banks support small populations of Swainson's thrush, veery, and warbling vireo. Large numbers of yellow warblers, varied thrushes, robins, willow fly-catchers, and red-eyed vireos nest in these trees. Swallows and king-fishers like to perch on the telephone wires that cross the Channel.

The water is flat and often blanketed with duckweed. Many parts of the Channel are very shallow. Species of waterfowl suited to the lush vegetation here include horned and eared grebes, pied-billed grebes, blue-winged teals and cinnamon teals, wood ducks, and ruddy ducks. The great blue heron commonly fishes in the Channel, even in winter. Heron tracks have been observed around the holes cut in the ice by fishermen. Painted turtles bask on semi-submerged logs, while mink, marten, raccoon, white-tailed deer—and sometimes moose—frequent the wooded banks of the Channel.

Annual spring floods once were devastating to many nesting species. Since 1968, however, the Wildlife Management Authority has built a network of interconnecting dykes and channels throughout the entire 7000 ha of protected wetland in the Creston Valley. Control of water levels and man-made nesting platforms and boxes have led to a wider variety of migrant species and a greater overall diversity of nesting waterfowl in the Valley.

A detailed guide, *Waterfowl in the Creston Valley*, was published in 1976 by the Wildlife Management Authority and the Canadian Wildlife Service to aid in species identification. An updated check-list of bird species is available at the Creston Valley Wildlife Centre. New entries are always welcome.

Distance: Duck Lake Channel, 12 km return Duck Lake, 4 km X 4 km.

Time: Estimate 4 km per hour, Duck Lake Channel, 3 hours.

Canoeing

Difficulty: Easy. Duck Lake is 2 to 3 m deep; the Channel is also shallow.

Canoe Access: South side of Duck Lake. Across from small parking area by pump-shed. Channel is also accessible from several places along Channel Road.

Parking: Small lot at pump-shed at end of Channel Road.

Maps: See Maps 1 and 4.

Photographs: Duck Lake—T. Patterson-Z.; Painted Turtle—Anonymous.

Note: Wildlife Management Unit land is open to hunters during the autumn hunting season, September to December.

Duck Lake

Painted Turtle

7. Rum Runner—
The Kootenay River from Porthill,
Idaho to the Old Ferry Landing

During Prohibition in the 1920s, rum used to run southward against the current of the Kootenay River, entering the United States illegally. Liquor-laden barges slipped past Customs, devoid of light, in the dead of night. The river may have since lost the thrill of its illicit activities, but it still provides great canoeing. This route will take you on a scenic tour of the Creston Valley via the river responsible for the area's geography. Follow the current for 18 km from Porthill, Idaho, to the Old Ferry Landing on Kootenay River Road.

Getting There

See Map 2—Two vehicles are needed for this one-way excursion. Park one vehicle at the Old Ferry Landing on the north shore of the River. To get there, turn west onto Kootenay River Road from Hwy 21, the highway on the west side of Creston that goes to the Unites States. Follow Kootenay River Road all the way to the River. This is the site of the Creston Yacht Club, which consists of a cement boat launch into the river, a wooden dock, and ample parking. There are no facilities here or anywhere along the river: no flush toilets, no fast food outlets, no garbage cans, no barbecue pits, no picnic tables. You are on your own. Please pack out what you pack in.

The second vehicle can be parked at Roy's Place in Porthill. Follow Hwy 21 south of Creston to the Canada-U.S. border. Report at U.S. Customs. Turn right at the first road in Idaho and go up the hill to Roy's Place. Roy's is an icon of American culture adorned with neon Schlitz and Coors signs--and is your last chance for facilities. There is a large parking area here. The launch is across the airstrip (airplanes have right-of-way) and consists of a cement ramp down into the river.

On The Water

Once the canoe is launched, follow the current northward back up to Canada. After less than 1 km, you must report to Canada Customs. There is a government dock and a walkway to the Customs building. You can ring up the officer from a telephone at the dock. Summer hours are 7 a.m. to 11 p.m.

(April to late October). Winter hours are 8 a.m. to 12 a.m. (late October to early April).

After clearing Customs, you will have 17 km of peaceful canoeing ahead of you. Except for the first 3 km and the last 1 km, all the land on the east side of the Kootenay River is owned by the Lower Kutenai Indian Band. A dyke borders the river on the west side for the entire length of this trip. Beyond the dyke is grazing and farm land. The river is wide and peaceful; the current is moderate; and there are no rapids or areas of rough water. It usually takes 4 to 5 hours of moderate paddling to reach the Old Ferry Landing. The Goat River converges with the Kootenay about 2 km from the Landing. Look for the dock and ramp on the north side of the river. The ferry has not been in service since 1965, when the Creston-Salmo Highway and new bridge were built.

The Kootenay River has its origins in the Rocky Mountains east of Invermere, B.C. It flows south into the United States where it is dammed at Libby, Montana. It then turns north and passes through Idaho and the Creston Valley, emptying into the deep and narrow, glacial-carved Kootenay Lake.

The river is home to several species of birds, animals, and fish. In addition to rainbow trout and whitefish, the bottom-dwelling sturgeon—almost prehistoric in appearance—inhabits the river in large numbers. The conservation officer in Creston reports fish caught to range in size from 80 lbs to 150 lbs (40 kg to 75 kg) and in age from 13 to 80 years old. The Wildlife branch has record of a 900 pounder caught by a Porthill resident. A current, joint study by British Columbia, Idaho, and Montana consists of collecting data and monitoring the sturgeon population in the Kootenay River.

Distance: 18 km.

Time: Estimate 4 km per hour, 4 to 5 hours.

Difficulty: Easy. Grade 1 river, minimal vertical drop, moderate current, with accessible banks in many places.

Canoe Access: Cement ramp across airstrip in Porthill, Idaho. Cement boat launch at the Old Ferry Landing.

Parking: Leave the first vehicle at the Old Ferry Landing on Kootenay River Road. Park second vehicle at Roy's Place, Porthill, Idaho. The trip begins here.

Canoeing

Maps: See Map 2.

Photographs: Canoe Launch at Roy's Place, Porthill, Idaho—T. Patterson-Z.; Aerial View of Kootenay River—C.V.W.M.A.

Note: Wildlife Management Unit land is open to hunters during the autumn hunting season, September to December.

Canoe Launch at Roy's Place, Porthill, Idaho

Aerial View of Kootenay River

8. Leach Lake and Channel

Leach Lake, contrary to implication, was not named after the slimy blood-sucker, but after a mysterious person named Leach. Few people know any-thing about Leach and more is known about the reservoir of water than its namesake.

Similar to Six Mile Slough, Leach Lake is a shallow body of water divided into 4 separate ponds by dykes. For the benefit of nesting waterfowl, the Wildlife Management Unit regulates the water level in the ponds by means of portals in the dykes.

Getting There

See Map 3—Follow Hwy 3 west from Creston and continue 4.3 km past the junction of Hwy 3 and Hwy 21. Turn north onto Nick's Island Road, the first road north after the silver bridge over the Kootenay River. Stay on Nick's Island Road for 4.4 km; the last 2 km are gravel, then dirt or mud, depending on the season. The hill you drive up and over is actually a dyke belonging to the Dyking District, a group of Creston Valley farmers. Because cattle are at large on the dyke, the fenced gate at the end of the road must be re-closed once you have passed through it. From the dyke, you can see the Old Kootenay River Channel join forces with the Kootenay River on the right. Park anywhere in the area and unload the canoe.

There are three navigable waterways to choose from:

1. The Kootenay River

The river is wide, quiet and peaceful; the current runs north. North of the launch, the land on the west side of the river is owned by the Wildlife Man-agement Area and is therefore more treed than the southern route. If you travel north, remember to allow more time for your return trip against the current.

2. The Channel

Paddle 0.2 km upstream on the Old Kootenay River Channel. Here a small tributary branches off to the north. About 0.1 km away is a dyke that must be portaged. The small channel continues up the entire length of Leach Lake Dyke, about 4 km. You must portage the dykes 4 more times in order to reach the Kootenay River. Watch for short-eared owls in the heavily treed area between the Channel and Leach Lake. Also watch for elk and white-tailed deer.

3. Leach Lake

To get to Leach Lake, turn north at the second tributary off the Old Kootenay River Channel. One portage over the dyke brings you to a small waterway which flows into Leach Lake about 0.5 km later. From Pond 1, you reach Ponds 2, 3, and 4 by portaging over the dykes dividing one pond from the next.

The ponds are ideal nesting habitats because the water is still, shallow, and covered with a mat of attractive, pink smartweed in the spring. Several nesting mounds have been constructed for the birds by the Wildlife Management Unit—and by the resident muskrats. Although the Management Unit does not openly discourage canoeing through these areas during the nesting months of May, June, and July, canoeists are encouraged to exercise care and caution. Since any disturbance to the birds is detrimental to nesting and breeding, please maintain a safe distance between you and the young families and occupied islands during late spring.

Distances: Many kilometres of waterway to explore.

Time: Estimate 4 km per hour.

Difficulty: Easy canoeing in the Channel and in Leach Lake. Some portaging necessary. No current; shallow water; accessible banks. Moderate canoeing in the River. Some current; banks not always accessible.

Canoe Access: At the end of Nick's Island North Road. Please close gate: cattle at large.

Parking: Grassy area adjacent to river.

Maps: See Maps 1, 3, and 4.

Photographs: Nesting Grebe—C.V.W.M.A.

Note: Wildlife Management Unit Land is open to hunters during the autumn hunting season, September to December.

A Nesting Grebe

Part Two
Bicycling

9. Farmland to Forest to Marshland

This is a 15 km loop beginning and ending at the Creston Valley Wildlife Centre. The route takes you past open farmland, through shaded hemlock and red cedar forest, and back to marshland where the Wildlife Centre is located.

Cycling on the highway should be avoided if there are children or novice cyclists in your group. As a major artery through southern British Columbia, Hwy 3 is subject to heavy traffic in the summer. Although the shoulder is paved, it is wide enough for only one bicycle at a time. The 4.7 km of highway cycling in this loop can be avoided by starting at the gas station on Nick's Island Road and finishing at the Wildlife Centre, providing you have two vehicles.

Getting There

See Map 3—Park at the Creston Valley Wildlife Centre located 1.2 km south of Hwy 3 on West Creston Road. On bicycle, retrace the 1.2 km back toward the highway. The road is paved, but has no shoulder.

It is amazing how much more you see, feel, hear and smell your surroundings using this mode of transportation. Birdlife is rich along this piece of road: herons, kingfishers, kestrels, and many waterfowl species can be sighted often. The belted kingfisher likes to perch on the telephone wire, spotting for fish in the creek beside the road. It will dive from its perch into the water with a resounding splash, returning to its wire with a small fish in its bill.

Yes, the *Turtle Crossing* sign is authentic. Watch for turtles, but do not help them cross the road. When picked up, turtles immediately lose their water. Female turtles need their water to lay eggs on the dry slope.

Turn right from West Creston Road onto Hwy 3 and ride for 4.7 km. From Hwy 3, turn right onto Nick's Island South Road, another paved secondary road without shoulders. Follow this road along the Kootenay River (3.8 km). The wooden bridge at the end of the road crosses over the Old Kootenay River Channel. From the bridge, you can see where the Channel joins the Kootenay River.

Along the roadside look for yellow tansy, goldenrod, and the white fruit of the snowberry in late summer. The last part of Nick's Island South Road is treed and shaded. White clematis vine, with its silky seed clusters (Old Men's Beards), grows in this wooded area by the road.

Turn right at the T-junction after the bridge and proceed west on West Creston Road. Cross a second wooden bridge over the Old Kootenay River Channel, and continue down the road. Cross the Corn Creek bridge, which marks kilometre 11 in the loop. West Creston Road then begins a wide turn to the north.

The next 3 km are up and down hills through stands of western red cedar, western hemlock, and grand fir. The final kilometre opens up to a vista of marshland owned and managed by the Creston Valley Wildlife Management Authority. In early spring, the rocky hillside on the left is yellow with glacier lilies. That odour, as you round the last corner, is of skunk cabbage. Related to taro, staple food of the Polynesians, skunk cabbage has the largest leaves of any plant in the Creston Valley. Also watch for garter snakes and turtles crossing the road on this last corner. Herons, Canada geese, teals, and mallards are usually found in the wet area on the right side. From the road, you can sometimes see owls in the tall, old cottonwoods across the wetland.

The Wildlife Centre is open daily during the summer months. It offers naturalist-led canoe trips and hikes, and a service for lending binoculars and field guides to visitors. It also has a display hall, a theatre, a small library, and a refreshment area—the Swallow's Nest.

Distance: 15 km.

Time: 1 1/2 hours.

Difficulty: Moderate. Some gentle hills, 4.7 km of highway, no shoulders on secondary roads.

Parking: Creston Valley Wildlife Centre.

Maps: See Map 3.

Photographs: Turtle Crossing, Wooden Bridge on West Creston Road—T. Patterson-Z.

Turtle Crossing, Wooden Bridge on West Creston Road

10. The Hill Climb

Only 5 km of this 17 km loop is uphill, with 5 km downhill and 7 km level. From the top of the climb, you have a wide-angle view of the Kootenay River and its green, rural valley.

Getting There

See Map 1—Follow Hwy 3 west from Creston. Turn right 0.2 km past the junction of Hwy 3 and Hwy 21 onto Lower Wynndel Road. Park in the large area by the turn-off.

Bicycle along Lower Wynndel Road to Hwy 3A. These first 7 km take you through grazing and farm lands. The seal-coated road on this flat section is not very smooth and has no shoulder; cycling this flat section warms up your muscles for the climb to come.

Pass Wynndel Box and Lumber and turn right onto Hwy 3A. Keep to the extra paved lane for slow traffic. The ride from the railroad tracks to the viewpoint takes about 20 minutes. This 5 km climb takes you past old apple orchards, a local potter's place, and the community of Wynndel.

A picnic shelter built at the summit of Hwy 3A by the Kiwanis Club marks kilometre 12. From this vantage point, you can see the tree-lined Kootenay River as it winds through the valley. This panoramic view also includes the Selkirk Mountains, which form the western border of the valley; Duck Lake, the small lake at the toe of Kootenay Lake to the north; and the edge of Kootenay Lake, which stretches another 75 km to the north.

See Map 3—The last 5 km take you downhill to Hwy 3, under the train bridge, and around a steeply-banked corner back to Lower Wynndel Road. You pass local rocksmith and woodcraftsman places, and an enclosure of Norwegian Fjord draft horses. At the first junction, turn right onto Hwy 3. Beware of the loose gravel shoulders.

Distance: 17 km.

Time: 1 hour.

Difficulty: Difficult. 5 km steep climb, no shoulders for most of the loop.

Parking: Lower Wynndel Road, off Hwy 3.

Maps: See Maps 1, 3, and 4.

Photographs: View from the Top of Hill Climb, Looking West—T. Patterson-Z.

View from the Top of Hill Climb, Looking West

11. Country Roads:
Erickson-Creston-Lister-Canyon-Erickson

This 25 km loop provides diversity: river crossings, hills up, hills down, hectic highway riding, quiet countryside, uncluttered orchards and crowded fruit stands. The secondary roads have no shoulders, and Hwy 3 has heavy traffic. Exercise caution on this loop.

Getting There

See Map 2—Begin anywhere along Hwy 3 in Erickson. Ride west to the boundary between Erickson and Creston. At the *Welcome to Creston* sign, turn left onto Sunset Boulevard. From Sunset, turn left onto 25 Avenue and follow it to the Erickson Back Road (Erickson Street on Map 5). Turn right onto the Erickson Back Road and travel downhill past the apple orchards and the home of Kokanee beer to Hwy 21. Tours through the brewery are available during the summer months.

Turn left onto Hwy 21; ride over the Goat River bridges; and continue 2 km to the Lower Kutenai Indian Band office and settlement. Turn left at Mallory Road, which is marked by golf course, airport, and guest ranch signs. Ride uphill for 1 km to the Creston Valley Golf Course. You have now completed nearly one-third of the total loop, 6.7 km.

Follow the Mallory Road onto 24 Street (see Map 2), and continue to the Canyon-Lister Road. Turn left onto the Canyon-Lister Road. Keep right past the Lister Firehall, following the Canyon-Lister Road to Canyon.

This second section of the loop provides scenic, low-stress cycling through the farming community of Lister. Hay and alfalfa embrace the senses along the route through the fields. Where Mallory Road becomes 24 Street, be sure to take time to enjoy the full-length view of the Skimmerhorns, part of the Purcell Range. The Canyon-Lister Road takes you uphill past orchards, small farms, and the Canyon store.

Pass the Canyon Park sign on the right. The road descends to the Canyon Bridge over the Goat River, which separates Canyon from Creston. Both Creston and Erickson are visible against the greenery of Goat Mountain. If you glance away from your front tire, you will see how Canyon got its name: the cliffs high above the churning Goat River are spectacular, especially in springtime when they are covered with fragrant mock orange shrubs.

In the 1930s, B.C. Hydro planned to dam Goat River at this location; the river now spills over the abandoned project, no longer needed after Hydro lines were put through Creston. After conquering the long hill up from the bridge, you may want to sample the apple cider from the big, cold keg at Littlejohn's fruit stand at the intersection of Canyon Road and Hwy 3.

Turn left onto Hwy 3 for the final one-third of the loop. Continue the uphill climb to Erickson, where zoning promotes agricultural development. Fruit stands along the highway give you an opportunity to sample the high-quality Erickson produce.

One plant that is common along the roadside throughout the entire loop, is chicory, also known as blue sailor. It is a hardy weed with light blue dandelion-like flowers that bloom from July to September. It is interesting to compare the appearance of the same patch of chicory in the morning and afternoon. On sunny and cloudy days alike, the flower heads turn inward at noon, appearing to close. With its flowers hidden, the plant seems to disappear. In the past, the tap root of the chicory has been used as a coffee additive and substitute, a practice more common in Europe than in North America.

Distance: 25 km.

Time: 3 1/2 hours.

Difficulty: Difficult. Some major climbs, uneven terrain, no shoulders on secondary roads, and heavy traffic on Hwy 3.

Parking: Along Hwy 3 in Erickson: Ponderosa Motel, Sunset Motel, Wayside Gardens, Wloka Fruit Stand, Bavarian Orchard Motel, Truscott's Fruit Stand, Kozy Tent and Trailer Campground.

Maps: See Map 2.

Photographs: Skimmerhorns—T. Patterson-Z.; The Apple Cider Keg at Littlejohn's—T. Patterson-Z.

The Apple Cider Keg at Littlejohn's

Skimmerhorns

12. River View

This is a 14 km loop through the Riverview District countryside. Visible from the loop are both the Goat River, with its steep canyonlike banks, and the Kootenay River, slowly meandering through the green valley. Beautiful scenery and variation in elevation make this loop especially interesting.

Getting There

See Map 2—Follow Hwy 21 south from Creston. Turn right about 1 km from the second Goat River bridge into a small parking area in front of the green rural post boxes. The bicycle loop begins across the highway on 40 Street.

Begin the loop with a healthy climb up 40 Street. Turn right onto Riverview Road. The Lower Kutenai Indian Band owns the land on the west side. Follow Riverview Road past 37th Street, past the Lower Kutenai Band's baseball diamond, and past the Rising Sun Guest Ranch. This B.C. government-approved ranch offers bed and breakfast to its guests, and trail and sleigh rides to the public. Be sure to book in advance if you plan to visit the ranch.

Riverview Road meets Mallory Road at a T-junction. Turn left onto Mallory Road and continue uphill past the Creston Valley Golf Course. Where Mallory Road becomes 24 Street, you can see the Skimmerhorns, part of the Purcell Range. The Rim Trail hike originates from the forestry and telecommunication towers atop Mount Thompson (elevation 2100 m). From the towers, you witness a stunning, panoramic view of the Kootenay Valley.

At the half-way point in the loop, 24 Street meets Sinclair Road. The intersection is marked by the old Lister School. Turn left onto Sinclair Road, and ride past the school, churchyard, and cemetery. Straight ahead is a view of Goat Mountain (elevation 1440 m), the unlogged watershed from which Creston's unchlorinated, mountain-clear water originates. There is a current controversy over this land as local logging companies want access to the forest. Two-thirds of the way up the mountain, there is a platform that hang-gliders use to take advantage of the updraft on clear summer days.

Turn left onto 28 Street, right onto Crestview, left onto 30 Street, then right onto Phillips. From here, you can glimpse the Goat River. Across the river are the urban area of Creston and the rural community of Erickson. Orchards are prevalent on the south-facing slopes. Cool nights combined with sunny days give Creston apples a high sugar content, rich colour, and flavour superior to apples grown elsewhere. Huscroft Lumber Mill is located to the east of the orchards.

Phillips runs downhill to 38 Street. Turn left onto 38 Street. This is the 10 km point in the loop. Follow 38 Street left onto 37 Street. Watch for lazuli buntings along the fencelines where the shrubbery is thick, and for eastern kingbirds nesting on the transformer boxes of the power poles. Hawks and kestrels cruise the open fields nearby.

At the end of 37 Street, turn right onto Riverview Road. This part of the loop gives the best view of Creston against Goat Mountain. To the west, the tree-lined Kootenay River moves peacefully from the Idaho boundary north to Kootenay Lake.

Riverview curves left onto 40th Street, taking the cyclist downhill to the stop sign at Hwy 21, across from the parking area.

Distance: 14.3 km.

Time: 1 1/2 hours.

Difficulty: Moderate. Some hills, no shoulder on secondary roads.

Parking: 1 km from second Goat River bridge on the west side of Hwy 21 in front of the green mail boxes.

Maps: See Map 2.

Photographs: Corn Harvest—Ralph McKone.

Corn Harvest

13. Apple Orchard Way

This 15-minute loop introduces the cyclist to some of the most beautiful orchard country in British Columbia. Take time to explore the spur roads off the Erickson Back Road. Half of the loop includes Hwy 3, a major artery through southern B.C. that is subject to heavy traffic in the summer. Although the shoulder is paved, it is wide enough for only one bicycle at a time. Children and novice cyclists should avoid cycling on the highway section.

Getting There

See Map 2—The loop can begin at any point along Hwy 3 in Erickson. Follow the highway east past the many fruit stands. The highway turns sharply to the south. Continue south onto Short Road (33 Avenue) past Fountain Grocery.

As you ride along Short Road, you can smell the apple orchards: MacIntosh, delicious, spartan, transparent, tydeman, and golden delicious are the main commercial varieties. Farmers are growing more dwarf and semi-dwarf trees for speed and ease in picking and spraying. The larger, older trees are more beautiful, but not as profitable as the small ones.

At the end of Short Road, turn right at the T-junction onto the Erickson Back Road (Erickson Street). In September, tractors pull flat-bed trailers full of stacked apple bins along this road. The bins are headed for the fruit packing shed located on Station Road. Most of the orchards along this road are apple, but pear, cherry, apricot, peach, and plum trees are also grown in Erickson.

See Map 5—From Erickson Street, turn right onto 25 Avenue, the boundary between Creston and Erickson, and continue north to Sunset Boulevard. Follow Sunset Boulevard—actually a short and narrow road—up to Hwy 3. Proceed east on the highway, back to your parked vehicle.

The unique climate and soils of Erickson lend themselves readily to fruit production. All who live and drive through the Creston Valley appreciate the fruit produced in this precious agricultural pocket of British Columbia.

Distance: 4.5 km.

Time: 1/4 hour.

Bicycling

Difficulty: Easy to Moderate. Traffic is heavy on Hwy 3. There are no shoulders on the secondary roads.

Parking: Along Hwy 3 in Erickson: Ponderosa Motel, Sunset Motel, Bavarian Orchard Motel, Wayside Gardens, Wloka Fruit Stand, Truscott's Fruit Stand, Kozy Tent and Trailer Campground, Fountain Grocery.

Maps: See Maps 2 and 5.

Photographs: Creston Peaches—R. McKone.

Creston Peaches

14. Duck Lake Dykes

The Creston Valley Wildlife Management Area is a federal-provincial project that has participation from private conservation agencies, such as *Ducks Unlimited*. A network of interconnecting dykes controls the amount and direction of water flow in the valley. Controlling water levels helps provide a suitable environment for waterfowl. The dykes make excellent cycling paths in spring and summer, and serve as platforms from which to view the waterfowl and wildlife.

Getting There

See Map 1—Turn right onto Lower Wynndel Road from Hwy 3. Turn left 6.9 km later onto Duck Lake Road. Watch for this sudden turn because it is not well marked. Pass the giant, pyramidal greenhouse on Duck Lake Road. Turn right at Arnold's Strawberry Farm onto Channel Road, 1.2 km from the beginning of Duck Lake Road.

See Map 4—Follow Channel Road for 5.5 km until a small pump-shed appears on the right. Park at the small area on the left and unload the bicycles.

There are 4 dykes to cycle:

1. Duck Lake Dyke
2. Duck Lake South Dyke
3. Kootenay River Dyke North
4. Kootenay River Dyke South

Times and distances indicate non-stop, return trips.

1. Duck Lake Dyke

Distance: 6 km.

Time: 1/2 hour.

This dyke has a well-packed gravel surface wide enough for only one vehicle. The dyke begins at the pump-shed and continues around the south end of Duck Lake, meeting the Kootenay River Dyke at a T-junction.

The dyke is also the northern border of the Duck Lake nesting area, where cattails, reeds, muskrat houses, and islands create a superlative nesting and breeding habitat for the many waterfowl species. Red-winged and yellow-headed blackbirds are plentiful in the reeds, and osprey can often be seen flying over the open water. Field species of birds can be observed on the last kilometre of the dyke: red-tailed and Cooper's hawks, American kestrels, savannah and lark sparrows, short-eared owls, and bald eagles. You may also see white-tailed deer, elk, or coyote in this field habitat.

2. Duck Lake South Dyke

Distance: 5.6 km.

Time: 1/2 hour.

From the parking area, retrace Channel Road for 1 km to a narrower, less travelled dyke on the right, Duck Lake South Dyke. This dyke borders the east and south sides of the nesting and breeding area. Birds are usually well hidden in the pond vegetation; chances of seeing them are good if you are very patient—or on stilts.

3. Kootenay River Dyke North

Distance: 17.2 km.

Time: 3 hours.

Follow Duck Lake Dyke its entire length to a T-junction. Kootenay River Dyke North begins at the T extending northward. This dyke leads to a pathway up to Hwy 3A. The return route is back to the parking area along the same path, beside the Kootenay River's east branch and via Duck Lake Dyke.

3a. Kootenay River Dyke North—long route

Distance: 30 km.

Time: 5 to 6 hours.

See map 1—A much longer, alternative route takes you back to the parking area via Hwy 3A, Lower Wynndel Road, Duck Lake Road, and Channel Road. The highway is narrow, winding, and congested in the summer. Shoulders here are gravel. Channel Road is loosely gravelled and dusty. If you do not mind dust and traffic, you will enjoy the scenery of this longer, more demanding route.

Built upon the eastern shore of the Kootenay River's east branch, Kootenay River Dyke North also borders the west and north sides of Duck Lake. Narrower than Duck Lake Dyke, Kootenay River Dyke North is well treed and has a great abundance of birdlife. Look for grey catbird, yellow warbler, eastern kingbird, Swainson's thrush, western tanager, cedar waxwing, American kestrel, and osprey. Two-thirds of the distance along the dyke is a heron rookery, a collection of more than thirty giant, great blue heron nests. The Wildlife Management Authority has constructed a blind to permit photography of the large birds without disturbing their nesting habits.

4. Kootenay River Dyke South

Distance: 5 km.

Time: 1/2 hour.

Follow Duck Lake Dyke its entire length to a T-junction. Kootenay River Dyke South begins at the T extending southward. Follow the dyke along the shore of the river to where the east and west branches of the Kootenay River meet. There is a waterfowl nesting and breeding area on the left as you ride. The return route is back to the parking area along the same path, beside the Kootenay River's east branch and via Duck Lake Dyke.

4a. Kootenay River Dyke South—long route

Distance: 8.8 km.

Time: 1 1/2 hours.

See Map 4—A longer, alternative route takes you past the canoe launch and onto Duck Lake Road. Turn north at Farmin Road. Turn right from Farmin Road onto the Duck Lake South Dyke, the dyke bordering the nesting area. At the end of Duck Lake South Dyke, turn left onto Channel Road and follow the road back to the parking area at the pump-shed.

Difficulty: Moderate. Dyke surfaces are rough. Mountain bikes would handle this terrain best.

Parking: At the end of Channel Road, across from the pump-shed.

Maps: See Maps 1 and 4.

Photographs: Cycling on the Duck Lake Dyke—T. Patterson-Z.

Note: Wildlife Management Unit land is open to hunters during the autumn hunting season, September to December.

Bicycling

Cycling on the Duck Lake Dyke

15. Summit Creek Dykes

From Summit Creek Campground to the Kootenay River, a collection of interconnecting dykes weave around tiny ponds and large areas of open water. Quiet, narrow channels meander through open wetland lined by tall, old cottonwoods along the Kootenay River. The dykes' rough, packed gravel surfaces are best travelled by mountain bike.

Getting There

See Map 3—Follow Hwy 3 west from Creston for 9 km. Turn right at Summit Creek Campground. Parking is available inside the campground, 0.5 km from the entrance, or just outside the gates. Park and unload the bikes. Cycle past the camping entrance and over the log bridge spanning Summit Creek; follow the Summit Creek Dyke road east. This dyke follows Summit Creek and the Old Kootenay River Channel, then branches north onto a dyke separating Leach Lake from a small, unnamed waterway that parallels the Kootenay River.

See Map 1—Smaller dykes, branching east from the main dyke, lead to the Kootenay River over the small channel. Small dyke roads also branch west through Leach Lake. About 6.6 km from the campground, the main dyke road comes to the Kootenay River.

The return journey is along the same dyke back to Summit Creek Campground. At the end of the dyke north, you may want to take the narrow, game trail that ascends the mountain on the west side of the dyke. (The trail is not marked on the maps.) This short trail meets the less travelled, upper part of the Dewdney Trail; it leads to the site of one of the Valley's old ferry landings used by the early white settlers. The hike may be somewhat overgrown and involve some bushwhacking.

Dykes have been built to divide Leach Lake into ponds for the purpose of enhancing the waterfowl nesting habitat. In conjunction with the ponds of Six Mile Slough and the ponds around the Wildlife Centre, one of the Leach Lake ponds is completely drained every seven years. This is called a *draw-down* by the Wildlife Management Authority: no water is allowed into the pond, which remains dry all summer. This action stops succession (forest overgrowth) and increases the productivity of the pond. The existing pond vegetation is allowed to die; new plants, encouraged to grow. New plant species in turn promote diversification of animal species that rely upon plant life for food. The draw-down effects complete renewal in the pond.

The Kokanee, a land-locked salmon, spawns in Summit Creek, where the clear, cool water is essential for the spawning process. In early September, the spawning red-backed Kokanee can be seen easily from the bridge and from the air, making the fish easy prey for eagles and ospreys. Also watch for species of fly-catcher and lazuli bunting in the trees that border Summit Creek.

Distance: 13.2 km.

Time: 1 1/2 hours.

Difficulty: Moderate. Rough dyke surfaces best covered by mountain bike.

Parking: Summit Creek Campground.

Maps: See Maps 1, 3, and 4.

Photographs: Summit Creek Dyke—T. Patterson-Z.

Note: Wildlife Management Unit land is open to hunters during the autumn hunting season, September to December.

The Summit Creek Dyke

16. Kootenay River Ferry Landing

Creston Valley was formerly the river-bottom of an earlier and broader Kootenay River. When the river waters receded, the valley was left with some of the most fertile farm land in the world. The Kootenay River Ferry Landing loop crosses part of the Valley, taking you along the former main highway of the area to the Old Ferry Landing. This ferry linked Creston to the rest of B.C. until 1965, when the Salmo-Creston skyway (Hwy 3) was completed.

Getting There

See Map 2—Travel south on Hwy 21 from the Hwy 3 junction toward the U.S. border and turn right onto Kootenay River Road. Look for a Pridham's Berry Farm sign painted with three strawberries. Turn right again immediately past the Hwy 21 turn-off and park on a small, flat piece of land belonging to Mr. Vern Petersen. Mr. Petersen generously permits visitors to park on his property. Although you could cycle to Kootenay River Road from Creston or Erickson, the return trip from Hwy 21 is an arduous climb (especially for young riders at the end of an 11 km bike ride).

Follow Kootenay River Road down to the Old Ferry Landing. The hard-packed gravel road passes fields of strawberries, blueberries, oats, timothy, apples, alfalfa hay, canola, wheat, and clover. Stacks of beehives pepper the clover fields. Half way along the straight, flat route to the Landing, you will see Agriculture Canada's research sub-station. Grain, forage crops, and fruit trees are arranged neatly in small plots. Straight ahead are the Selkirk Mountains; to the north, the bridge spanning the Kootenay River. Watch for songbirds singing in the rose hedges. Once you arrive at the Kootenay River, you may see people fishing at the dock for rainbow trout, whitefish, large-mouthed bass, and, on rare occasion, for sturgeon.

The wide Creston Valley attracts many species of prairie bird not usually found in a mountain community: meadow-larks, bobolinks, and magpies. Other birds commonly seen from the road include mourning doves, ring-necked pheasants, killdeers, and flickers. Late in the summer, red-tailed hawks or marsh hawks sit atop the telephone poles.

The return trip presents a flattering view of Creston ascending Goat Mountain, with the Purcell Range (elevation 2100 m) behind.

Distance: 11 km.

Time: 1 hour.

Difficulty: Easy. Rough road surface.

Parking: Mr. Vern Peterson's property.

Maps: See Map 2.

Photographs: Kootenay River ferry landing—T. Patterson-Z.

Kootenay River ferry landing

Part Three
Walking

17. Wloka Orchard

To capture the essence of the Creston Valley, take a walk through an apple orchard. Catch a glimpse of the orchard farmer's lifestyle and let the kids watch the apples grow.

Getting There

See Map 2—Wloka Orchard is located just behind the Wloka family's fruit stand on the north side of Hwy 3, across from Wayside Gardens. The fruit stand can be reached on foot from many of the motels along Hwy 3. Parking is also available at the fruit stand.

The Wlokas have 13.6 acres of apple orchard. Most of the apples are a Spartan variety that ripens in late September. Every fourth tree in every second row is a Tydeman apple, which ripens in late August. The Tydemans are included for variety and for the cross-pollination that helps each tree produce a larger crop. The climate of the Creston Valley is ideal for apple-growing. Clear sunny days combined with cool nights give the apples a high natural sugar content, rich colour, and unbeatable flavour.

The view of Creston Valley from the top of the orchard is rewarding: you can see the districts of Lister and Canyon to the south, the beautiful Purcell Mountains to the east, and the Selkirk Mountains to the west. Wloka Orchard and the several other orchards visible from here are located in the district of Erickson.

Try some of the home-grown fruit before you leave the Valley. It is more tasty and succulent than imported produce because it is fresher.

Before you set out on your walk, the Wlokas ask that you report at the fruit stand for information concerning spray days and wildlife in the orchard (e.g., black bears).

Distance: 1 1/2 km.

Time: 1/2 hour.

Difficulty: Moderate. Uneven ground, uphill one way, downhill to return.

Parking: Wlokas' Fruit Stand on Hwy 3.

Maps: See Map 2.

Photographs: September Macs—T. Patterson-Z.

September Macs

18. Duck Lake and Nesting Area

The Creston Valley Wildlife Management Unit owns and manages 7000 hectares of the Creston Valley for the purpose of waterfowl and wildlife protection and preservation. Since 1968, a network of dykes has been developed to protect much of the wetland from spring flooding. These dykes also benefit the birdwatcher by serving as a platform from which to view resident and visiting bird species. The dykes around Duck Lake and the nesting area are possibly the very best locations in the Valley for birdwatching.

Getting There

See Map 1—Follow Hwy 3 west from Creston. Turn right onto Lower Wynndel Road from Hwy 3, and turn left 6.9 km later onto Duck Lake Road. Pass the giant, pyramidal greenhouse and turn north onto Channel Road at Arnold's Strawberry Farm.

See Map 4—Follow Channel Road for 5.5 km until a pump-shed appears on the right side of the road. Park in the clearing on the left.

Once past the pump-shed, you are on the Duck Lake Dyke. The dyke road curves west and separates Duck Lake from the lush vegetation of the nesting area. The waterfowl listed below have been spotted in and around this area.

The last kilometre of the dyke turns away from the Lake and crosses part of a field. The field bird species seen from here are red-tailed hawk, American kestrel, savannah sparrow, lark sparrow, short-eared owl, and bald eagle. Duck Lake Dyke meets the Kootenay River Dyke at a T-junction. Beyond the dyke is the east branch of the Kootenay River. The following bird species have been sighted at the T-junction: western tanagers, grey catbirds, yellow warblers, eastern kingbirds, Swainson's thrushes, cedar waxwings, American kestrels, and ospreys.

The Creston Valley Wildlife Management Authority and Canadian Wildlife Service have issued a field guide called *Waterfowl in the Creston Valley*. It displays all the nesting and migrant species of waterfowl that have been seen in this area. Since the book's publication in 1976, eight more waterfowl species have begun nesting here. The following is an updated list:

Common loon
Red-necked grebe *
Horned grebe *
Western grebe *

Walking

Clark's grebe
Pied-billed grebe *
Tundra swan
Canada goose *
White-fronted goose
Snow goose
Mallard *
Gadwall *
American widgeon *
Pintail *
Green-winged teal *
Blue-winged teal *
Cinnamon teal *
Wood duck *
Redhead *
Ring-necked duck
Canvasback *
Greater scaup
Lesser scaup
Common goldeneye *
Barrow's goldeneye
Bufflehead *
Harlequin duck
Ruddy duck *
Hooded merganser *
Common merganser *
American coot *

* Have been known to nest in the area.

Distance: 6 km, along Duck Lake Dyke return.

Time: 4 1/2 hours.

Difficulty: Easy.

Parking: At the end of Channel Road across from pump-shed.

Maps: See Maps 1 and 4.

Photographs: Birdwatching from Dyke—Government of British Columbia; Tundra Swans: Spring Migration—C.V.W.M.A.

Note: Wildlife Management Area land is open to hunters during the autumn hunting season, September to December.

Walking

Birdwatching from the Dyke

Tundra Swans

19. The Heron Rookery

Here is your opportunity to see great blue herons nesting in trees. The rookery is a collection of more than thirty large, rather flat nests. The nests are made of branches, twigs, and reeds, and are repaired annually in early spring. In April before the trees have leaves, adult birds can be seen sitting on or flying over the clearly visible nests. Usually seen standing on one of their long legs in shallow water, these birds with metre-long wing spans appear unusually awkward in their nests atop the tall trees. To facilitate photography of the birds and to protect them from human intrusion at nesting time, the Wildlife Management Unit has constructed a blind in this area.

Getting There

See Map 1—Follow Hwy 3A (also known as the Kootenay Lake Road) north from Creston. This road leads to the ferry across Kootenay Lake and on to Nelson.

See Map 4—Pass through the community of Wynndel and continue for another 12 km on Hwy 3A. The elevation of the highway permits views of Duck Lake Channel, Duck Lake Dyke, and the open water of Duck Lake. Duck Lake Dyke serves as the dividing line between the Lake and the nesting area.

Follow Hwy 3A past the community of Sirdar and the Imasco rock-crushing plant. Park in the area on the right side of Hwy 3A less than 1 km past the Imasco sign. Cross the highway and follow the path that starts at the white fence. This path leads across the C.P.R. tracks, past a pump-shed, and up onto the Kootenay River Dyke.

The water near the pump-shed becomes free of ice earlier in spring than the rest of Duck Lake. For this reason, you may see many bird species in this relatively small area early in the March thaw.

Follow the dyke road for 1 1/2 km. Turn onto the foot-path that appears where the dyke road begins to curve southward. Follow this path through the rose bushes, red osier dogwood, and tall grass to the Kootenay River. A blind made of red osier dogwood is on the river's edge.

The huge heron nests across the river in the tops of the old cottonwood trees are full of activity in April and May, but the area is still interesting in the summer. Herons abound in the shallows of Duck Lake and along the margins of the river. Herons eat fish, frogs, salamanders, water snakes, and large insects.

South of the dyke is Duck Lake, a large, shallow body of water teeming with birdlife. Moose have also been seen grazing up to their bellies in the cattails along the shore. Muskrats like this environment as well. North of the dyke, osprey and eagles perch in the poplar trees guarding the bank of the east branch of the Kootenay River, which flows quietly northward into Kootenay Lake.

Kootenay River Dyke continues southward past the rookery, separating Duck Lake from the east branch of the Kootenay River for another 7 km.

Distance: 3.2 km.

Time: 2 1/2 hours.

Difficulty: Easy.

Parking: Extension of shoulder off Hwy 3A.

Maps: See Maps 1 and 4.

Photographs: Hikers on the Trail to the Heron Rookery—T. Patterson-Z.

Hikers on the Trail to the Heron Rookery

20. Wayside Gardens

Wayside Gardens is the work of Mr. William Peters, who came to Creston from northern Alberta. In 1964, Mr. Peters purchased ten acres of woodland on a hillside and began his project. Amazingly, only a handful of people designed and constructed the entire garden: Mr. and Mrs. Peters, dedicated and knowledgeable friends and staff, and one very energetic, strong-backed father-in-law.

Getting there

See Map 2—This popular garden is probably the most scenic picnic area you will find in the Kootenays.

The Garden Walk

This walk takes you through artfully combined natural and man-made landscapes edged by apple orchards. Wayside Gardens is one of the most beautiful spots in the Creston Valley year round. Daffodils, tulips, and crocuses are a colourful welcome to spring after a black and white winter. Spring flowering trees include cherry, plum, crabapple, magnolia, catalpa, linden, tulip, and flowering quince.

In late spring, Wayside Gardens has the greatest variety and number of rhododendrons east of the Coast Mountains. With the aid of a natural stand of birch, Mr. Peters has created the protected, acidic environment especially conducive to the growth of these broad-leaved evergreens.

In summer, you can view hundreds of hybrid tea roses from the hand-crafted gazebo at the crest of the hill. Autumn creates a spectacle of colour. The perfectly smooth white bark of the Himalayan Birch in a sea of gold contrasts beautifully with the intense blue of an October sky.

The Wayside Gardens is pleasant place to spend an afternoon: the teahouse at the entry gate provides refreshment, and picnic tables have been set on the lawns for the bag-lunch crowd. Occasionally, the choir drops in for a sing; and, from time to time, wedding vows are exchanged in the peacefulness of the garden.

Distance: The gardens comprise 5 acres.

Time: You will want to take time to enjoy the beauty of the gardens.

Difficulty: Easy. Wheelchair accessible.

Parking: At the garden gate entrance.

Maps: See Map 2.

Photographs: Himalayan Birch at the Wayside Gardens—T. Patterson-Z.

Note: There is an entrance fee.

Himalayan Birch at the Wayside Gardens

21. The Dewdney Trail

In 1863, the Rush was on. Gold had been discovered in the East Kootenays. The sudden need to connect Hope to the gold fields of Wild Horse Creek (20 km north of Cranbrook) brought Edgar Dewdney to the region. Dewdney was hired by Governor Seymour to find an all-Canadian route to Wild Horse Creek so that Canadians could avoid U.S. Customs delays.

This walk takes you along part of Dewdney's original trail used by mules and packhorses to transport supplies and minerals. The trail takes you from lush lowland forest, through semi-open meadow, and up to dry mountain forest. Along the trail to Williams Creek Falls, you can easily view Leach Lake and the Purcell Mountains to the east.

Getting There

See Map 1—Follow Hwy 3 west from Creston across the flats toward Summit Creek. Turn right into Summit Creek Campground, 1.2 km past the Wildlife Centre exit. Parking is available 0.5 m from the campground's gate.

See Map 3—The trail begins at the suspension bridge over Summit Creek. In September, the Kokanee salmon spawn in great numbers in this creek. The Kokanee attract many osprey and other fish-eating birds, which in turn bring many wildlife photographers to the creek.

The trail is marked with flagging tape and maintains a northern direction along the side of Midgeley Mountain. The vegetation here is thick; the air, heavy with moisture. In June, the mock orange shrub is in bloom. Besides having a pretty, white, four-petalled flower, this shrub has a lovely aroma similar to that of the orange blossom.

Where wetland meets dry mountain slope, you will see a wide variety of plants, birds, and animals. At Shorty Bolton's cabin, a favourite skunk hideout, the trail opens up to meadow and mountainside. Watch for western tanagers. With the warmth and moisture of the eastern exposure, flowers usually bloom here first. In April and May, the glacier lilies may be so thick that they form a yellow mat. White springbeauty blooms at the same time of year, but is often hidden by dead grass.

Later in the year, these same slopes are occupied by ox-eye daisy, evening primrose, and yellow salsify (goatsbeard). The small, dark brown rubber boa basks in the heat where the slope is especially sunny and sandy. This snake is a distant relative to the larger boa, constricting its prey in a similar manner, though on a reduced scale.

The drumming of ruffed grouse can be heard along the path in spring. High points along the trail provide excellent views of the feeding and resting waterfowl around Leach Lake.

There are signs of earlier human habitation below Williams Creek Falls. This might have been a stopping place on the Dewdney Trail where fresh water was readily available. Some old logs are arranged where buildings may have existed. Non-native species of lilac and rhubarb grow around the logs; someone from the distant past must have brought them here.

The original Dewdney Trail continues 4 km past the Falls to the Kootenay River. This section of the trail is rough and fragmented. If you plan to continue along the Trail past Williams Creek Falls, consider bringing with you some knowledge of the area, a detailed map, a compass, and bear bells.

The view of the Creston Valley has changed a great deal since Dewdney's time. In 1863, you would have looked out onto a vast swamp infested with mosquitos. Today, the dyked farm land and managed wetland look like the patchwork quilt that Dewdney might have wished he had had.

Distance: 5 km, Williams Creek Falls return.

Time: 4 hours.

Difficulty: Moderate.

Parking: Summit Creek Campground.

Maps: See Maps 1 and 3.

Photographs: The Suspension Bridge over Summit Creek—T. Patterson-Z.

The Suspension Bridge over Summit Creek

22. Lone Pine Hill

This 1 1/2-hour hike incorporates dry mountainside, open meadow, and wetland habitats—each with its own resident flora and fauna. A panoramic view of the Creston Valley is yours to absorb from the top of Lone Pine Hill: fertile farmland, the peaceful Kootenay River, orchards, the Purcell Range, and the town of Creston against Goat Mountain.

Getting There

See Map 3—Follow Hwy 3 west from Creston for 9 km. Turn left onto West Creston Road and travel to the Creston Valley Wildlife Centre. Park at the Wildlife Centre and walk 0.8 km south along West Creston Road to a small bridge on the left. Across from the bridge on the right (west) side of the road, the trail up to Lone Pine Hill begins.

The trail ascends steeply to a meadow. In spring, you pass through a profusion of yellow glacier lilies. The dry slope houses Nashville warblers, rufous hummingbirds, common nighthawks, rufous-sided towhees, western tanagers, ospreys, long-eared owls, great horned owls, and barred owls. At your feet, you may see garter snakes and rubber boas. The rubber boa is distinguished from the garter snake by its solid deep brown colour; and, like the boa constrictor, the rubber boa constricts its prey.

Observe the Creston Valley from the top of the hill. Seated at the bench near the lone ponderosa pine tree, you will enjoy a scenic view and be able to detect the historical geography of the valley. Note the U-shape of the Kootenay Valley when you look north to Kootenay Lake. A smaller, "hanging" U-shaped valley to the northeast near Wynndel seems to be suspended above the community. Glaciers carved these round-edged geological formations.

Now look west to the sharp V-shaped valleys against the mountainside. These valleys were formed by running water--a much quicker geological process than the glaciation that formed the U-shaped valleys. The nearest existing glacier to the Creston Valley is Kokanee Glacier, 60 km up Kootenay Lake, which is visible from Hwy 3A as you board the ferry to the Selkirk side of Kootenay Lake.

Over a short distance, the trail takes you from sunny, open meadow down to the cool, damp forest of Benny's Creek. You will feel that the change in climate has been quick as you follow the mushroomed trail beneath birch and western larch trees. Continue along the creek up to where the rock cliff overlooks the trail. You will see wild, climbing blue clematis; honeysuckle; and red-stemmed dogbane as you hike; and possibly alligator lizards and blue-tailed skunks as well.

On your return to the Wildlife Centre along West Creston Road, look for skunk cabbage, toadflax, Jacob's ladder, yarrow, butter and eggs, chicory, common mullein, and ox-eye daisy--common roadside plants.

Distance: 2 km.

Time: 1 1/2 hours.

Difficulty: Moderate.

Parking: Wildlife Centre.

Maps: See Map 3.

Photographs: Osprey-eye View from Lone Pine Hill—C.V.W.M.A.

Osprey-eye View from Lone Pine Hill

23. Corn Creek Woods

Approximately 3 km south of the Wildlife Centre, a trail leads into the quiet shade of Corn Creek Woods. The trail parallels the Old Kootenay River Channel for a short distance and then emerges into open wetland in view of the Wildlife Centre. This walk offers an opportunity to observe plant and bird life in three different habitats: forest, riverside, and wetland.

Getting There

See Map 3—Follow Hwy 3 west from Creston to the Wildlife Centre turn-off. Turn south onto West Creston Road and travel 2.9 km past the Wildlife Centre parking lot. Turn left onto a small roadway and park in front of the Wildlife Management Authority silver fence; there is only enough space to park one or two vehicles.

Cross the wooden sty over the fence. The main trail is just south of the sty. It follows the gas pipeline and borders the jumbled waterway of Corn Creek. This trail is more open and easier to follow than some of the tiny game trails through the woods. These smaller trails, like the one leading straight ahead of the sty, take you through the deeper, darker parts of the forest.

The forest is made up of western red cedar, western hemlock, Douglas fir, and grand fir. In the deep woods where light barely penetrates, you are likely to see Indian pipestem, a ghostly-looking plant lacking chlorophyll. Indian pipestem is a saprophyte: that is, a plant nourished by decaying plant matter. A second saprophytic plant, pine drops, can be found in the humus of the surrounding coniferous forest. Look on the ground for the pine drops' red stems which carry forty to sixty little white heather-like flowers. While investigating the forest flora, look also for squirrels, grouse, woodpeckers, and great horned owls.

The trail leads out of the woods to the Old Kootenay River Channel, a slow-moving body of water flanked by tall, old poplar trees. These trees are used by the herons, osprey, and eagles in the area. Elk, white-tailed deer, black bears, and coyotes prefer the open grassy areas, whereas mink and muskrats like the cover along the river's edge. Black bears frequent the trail, so be alert at all times for bear sign; carry bear bells with you.

The final stretch of the trail takes you along a grass-covered dyke back to West Creston Road through untreed, open wetland. The wetland is home to rails, bitterns, coots, black terns, king birds, swallows, snipes, kingfishers, red-winged and yellow-headed blackbirds, and many species of waterfowl.

A black-crowned night heron has been spotted in one of the man-made ponds. Inactive during the day, this stalky, short-necked heron prefers to fish at night.

The dyke leads back to West Creston Road, where a V-space in the fence allows hikers to exit. The parking area is 1.7 km north along West Creston Road from here. Flowers you might see along the roadside include sweet clover, chicory, forget-me-not, ox-eye daisy, and nightshade. This last plant is a vine with purple, shooting star-shaped flowers and scarlet fruit that resembles a miniature tomato. This local variety of nightshade is related to the deadly nightshade, a plant similar in appearance which has very toxic immature fruit.

Distance: 6 km.

Time: Estimate 1 1/4 km per hour, 4 1/2 hours.

Difficulty: Easy.

Parking: 2.9 km south of Wildlife Centre on West Creston Road.

Maps: See Map 3.

Photographs: Nesting boxes in Corn Creek Woods—T. Patterson-Z.

Note: Wildlife Management Unit land is open to hunters during the autumn hunting season, September to December.

Nesting boxes in the Corn Creek Woods

24. Schikurski Park
and other Park and Picnic Places

Schikurski Park (Regina Street)

Schikurski Park on Regina Street preserves a small pocket of natural landscape against a rocky outcropping. The vegetation found here is native to the area.

A walking trail takes you through 1.3 hectares of wooded areas, moss-covered rocks, steep banks, and open, grassy (frisbee-throwing) areas. There are some picnic tables in a quiet copse of aspen trees. The leaves make great fun in the fall. A small creek cuts through the park and disappears into a stand of willow trees native to the area. The abundance of trees and shrubbery in the park houses an abundance of bird and animal life. There is no playground equipment, but children will find it easy to get involved with nature at Schikurski Park. Plans for a fitness trail adjacent to the Park are in the works.

Centennial Park (Erickson Street and 11 Avenue)

See Map 5—This park has play apparatus for kids: well-constructed, solid climbing equipment, slides, swings, and monkey bars. There is also a picnic shelter with washrooms, drinking fountains, picnic tables, benches, and plenty of tall, shade-bearing trees. The ball diamond at this park hosts Creston's fastball leagues in spring and summer.

Kinsmen Park (Cedar Street and 22 Avenue)

See Map 5—Kinsmen Park plans major renovation in the future. At present, the park has some dated playground equipment, a ball diamond, and tennis courts. Two more asphalt-surfaced tennis courts are located at the Prince Charles Secondary School on 16th Avenue and Dogwood Street.

Don Burns (Elm Street and 25 Avenue)

See Map 5—Here is a small park with trees, picnic tables, a small shelter and washrooms. Children's play equipment consists of a basketball net and three swings.

Summit Creek Campground

See Map 3—Follow Hwy 3 west from Creston for 9 km. Summit Creek Campground is 1.2 km past the Wildlife Centre turn-off. There are two picnic areas here: one close to the campground in the tall cedar trees; the second near the suspension bridge in an open area. The mixed deciduous/coniferous forest along the banks of Summit Creek is home to many species of birdlife, including Swainson's thrush, winter wren, hammond's fly-catcher, lazuli bunting, ruffed grouse, American kestrel, pileated woodpecker, blue jay, stellar's jay, and warbling and red-eyed vireos. Ospreys have nested near the suspension bridge in the picnic area. Dippers, belted kingfishers, and spotted sandpipers may be seen along the creek. In September, the spawning, red-backed Kokanee salmon are visible from the bridges.

There are 2 hiking trails at the campground area:

1. Summit Creek Woods trail is a small loop beginning and ending at Campsite #39.

2. The Dewdney Trail begins at the suspension bridge and continues northward 2.5 km to Williams Creek Falls. The hike is described earlier in this guide.

Wayside Gardens

See Map 2—This is probably the most scenic picnic area you will find in the Kootenays. There is a teahouse on the grounds, but you are welcome to bring your own lunch and use the picnic tables on the lawns between the flowering crabapple and fragrant linden trees. Because Wayside Gardens is a quiet, restful place, not designed for active play, there is no playground apparatus for children. This is a garden where every tree, bush and flower receives loving attention.

Photographs: Aspen Grove in Early Spring, Schikurski Park—T. Patterson-Z.; Tire Swing at Centennial Park—T. Patterson-Z.

Tire Swing at Centennial Park